KEEP
CALM

YOU'RE ONLY

60

KEEP CALM YOU'RE ONLY 60

With text contributed by Vicky Edwards

Summersdale Publishers Ltd
46 West Street
Chichester
West Sussex
PO19 1RP
UK

www.summersdale.com

Printed and bound in the Czech Republic

ISBN: 978-1-84953-224-2

Substantial discounts on bulk quantities of Summersdale books are available to corporations, professional associations and other organisations. For details contact Summersdale Publishers by telephone: +44 (0) 1243 771107, fax: +44 (0) 1243 786300 or email: nicky@summersdale.com.

KEEP
CALM

YOU'RE ONLY

60

summersdale

CONTENTS

ANOTHER
YEAR
OLDER

I'm 60 years of age. That's
16 Celsius!

George Carlin

You're not 60. You're 18 with 42 years of experience.

Anonymous

A diplomat is a man who always remembers a woman's birthday but never remembers her age.

Robert Frost

The best birthdays
of all are those that
haven't arrived yet.

Robert Orben

On the last day of my 59th year I was trembling with anticipation. I've heard so much about the swinging sixties – I couldn't wait to get stuck in!

Anonymous

Some people
reach the age of 60
before others.

Lord Hood

I was always taught to respect my elders and I've now reached the age when I don't have anybody to respect.

George Burns

For all the advances in medicine, there is still no cure for the common birthday.

John Glenn

Our birthdays are feathers in the broad wing of time.

Jean Paul Richter

From our birthday,
until we die,
Is but the winking of an eye.

W. B. Yeats,
To Ireland in the Coming Times

Whatever with the past has gone, the best is always yet to come.

Lucy Larcom

My wife hasn't had a birthday in four years. She was born in the year of Lord-only-knows.

Anonymous

If we could be twice
young and twice old
we could correct all
our mistakes.

Euripides

Every year on your
birthday, you get a
chance to start new.

Sammy Hagar

I have everything I had 20 years ago, only it's all a little bit lower.

Gypsy Rose Lee

You can't turn back the clock. But you can wind it up again.

Bonnie Prudden

JUST
WHAT
I
ALWAYS
WANTED

A hug is the perfect gift;
one size fits all, and nobody
minds if you exchange it.

Anonymous

Youth is the gift of nature, but age is a work of art.

Garson Kanin

You know you are
getting old when the
candles cost more
than the cake.

Bob Hope

We know we're getting old
when the only thing we want
for our birthday is not to be
reminded of it.

Anonymous

Yesterday is history,
tomorrow is a mystery, but
today is a gift. That is why it
is called the present.

Eleanor Roosevelt

Last week the candle factory burned down. Everyone just stood around and sang 'Happy Birthday'.

Steven Wright

At my age the best gift one can hope for is a continuing sense of humour. The ability to laugh, especially at ourselves, keeps the heart light and the mind young.

Anonymous

There are 364 days
when you might get
un-birthday presents...
and only one for
birthday presents,
you know.

Lewis Carroll,
Through the Looking Glass

All the world is a birthday cake, so take a piece, but not too much.

George Harrison

A true friend
remembers your
birthday but not
your age.

Anonymous

A friend never defends
a husband who gets
his wife an electric
skillet for her birthday.

Erma Bombeck

Birthdays are good for you.
Statistics show that the
people who have the most
live the longest.

Larry Lorenzoni

A birthday is just the first day of another 365-day journey around the sun. Enjoy the trip.

Anonymous

GRIN
AND
BEAR
IT

Sixty is the new forty!

Bill Maher

Getting old is a bit like
getting drunk; everyone else
looks brilliant.

Billy Connolly

I still have a full deck; I just
shuffle slower now.

Anonymous

Age is a matter of
feeling, not of years.

George William Curtis

Men are like wine.
Some turn to vinegar,
but the best improve
with age.

C. E. M. Joad

At my age I do what Mark Twain did. I get my daily paper, look at the obituaries page and if I'm not there I carry on as usual.

Patrick Moore

Old age is an excellent time for outrage. My goal is to say or do at least one outrageous thing every week.

Maggie Kuhn

Age is an issue of mind over matter. If you don't mind, it doesn't matter.

Mark Twain

It's sad to grow old,
but nice to ripen.

Brigitte Bardot

My idea of Hell is to be young again.

Marge Piercy

I so enjoy waking up and not having to go to work. So I do it three or four times a day.

Gene Perret

One of the best parts of growing older? You can flirt all you like since you've become harmless.

Liz Smith

There is always a lot to be thankful for, if you take the time to look. For example, I'm sitting here thinking how nice it is that wrinkles don't hurt.

Anonymous

No matter what happens, I'm loud, noisy, earthy and ready for much more living.

Elizabeth Taylor

Time and trouble will tame
an advanced young woman,
but an advanced old woman
is uncontrollable by any
earthly force.

Dorothy L. Sayers

I'm not interested in age. People who tell me their age are silly. You're as old as you feel.

Elizabeth Arden

DO
A LITTLE
DANCE
MAKE
A LITTLE
LOVE

Grow old along with me! The
best is yet to be.

Robert Browning

The more you praise and
celebrate your life, the more
there is in life to celebrate.

Oprah Winfrey

Let us celebrate the occasion with wine and sweet words.

Titus Maccius Plautus

Old people aren't exempt
from having fun and
dancing... and playing.

Liz Smith

It's important to have a twinkle in your wrinkle.

Anonymous

I always make a point of
starting the day at 6 a.m. with
champagne. It goes straight
to the heart and cheers one
up. White wine won't do. You
need the bubbles.

John Mortimer

A man of 60 has spent
20 years in bed and
over three years
in eating.

Arnold Bennett

Old age is always 15 years older than I am.

Bernard M. Baruch

With mirth and laughter let
old wrinkles come.

William Shakespeare,
The Merchant of Venice

I'd hate to die with a good liver, good kidneys and a good brain. When I die I want everything to be knackered.

Hamish Imlach

There comes a time
in every woman's life
when the only thing
that helps is a glass
of champagne.

Bette Davis

If you give up smoking, drinking and loving, you don't actually live longer, it just seems longer.

Clement Freud

The older I get, the
more I realise that just
keeping on keeping on
is what life's all about.

Janis Ian

There is no pleasure
worth forgoing just for
an extra three years in
the geriatric ward.

John Mortimer

Age does not diminish the extreme disappointment of having a scoop of ice cream fall from the cone.

Jim Fiebig

The ageing process has you firmly in its grasp if you never get the urge to throw a snowball.

Doug Larson

YOUNG
AT
HEART

Although it sounds absurd, it is true to say I felt younger at 60 than I felt at 20.

Ellen Glasgow

They say genes skip generations. Maybe that's why grandparents find their grandchildren so likeable.

Joan McIntosh

There is no old age.
There is, as there
always was, just you.

Carol Matthau

My grandmother started
walking five miles a day
when she was 60. She's
97 now, and we don't know
where the hell she is.

Ellen DeGeneres

Ageing seems to be
the only available way
to live a long life.

Kitty O'Neill Collins

I didn't get old on purpose,
it just happened. If you're
lucky it could happen to you.

Andy Rooney

Grandchildren don't
make a man feel old;
it's the knowledge
that he's married to
a grandmother.

G. Norman Collie

An old timer is one who remembers when we counted our blessings instead of our calories.

Anonymous

Old age isn't so bad when you consider the alternative.

Maurice Chevalier

I'm not young enough
to know everything.

Oscar Wilde

Men do not quit
playing because they
grow old; they grow
old because they
quit playing.

Oliver Wendell Holmes Sr

Inside every older person
is a younger person –
wondering what the
hell happened.

Cora Harvey Armstrong

We are always the
same age inside.

Gertrude Stein

It takes a long time to
become young.

Pablo Picasso

Old age is no place
for sissies.

Bette Davis

With 60 staring me in the face, I have developed inflammation of the sentence structure and a definite hardening of the paragraphs.

James Thurber

OLDER
AND
WISER?

They told me if I got older
I'd get wiser. In that case I
must be a genius.

George Burns

If you are 60 years old
and have no regrets,
you haven't lived.

Christy Moore

The older I grow the more I distrust the familiar doctrine that age brings wisdom.

H. L. Mencken

You are only young
once, but you can
be immature for
a lifetime.

John P. Grier

The secret to staying young
is to live honestly, eat
slowly, and lie about
your age.

Lucille Ball

I live in that solitude
which is painful in
youth, but delicious in
the years of maturity.

Albert Einstein

The mind that is wise
mourns less for what age
takes away; than what it
leaves behind.

William Wordsworth

Age is a high price to pay for maturity.

Tom Stoppard

Becoming a grandmother
is wonderful. One moment
you're just a mother. The
next you are all-wise
and prehistoric.

Pam Brown

We are young only
once, after that
we need some
other excuse.

Anonymous

One of the good things
about getting older is
that you find you're more
interesting than most of the
people you meet.

Lee Marvin

Experience is the
name everyone gives
to their mistakes.

Oscar Wilde

I don't want to retire.
I'm not that good at
crossword puzzles.

Norman Mailer

The first hundred years are the hardest.

Wilson Mizner

If I had my life to live over again, I would make the same mistakes, only sooner.

Tallulah Bankhead

When I was a boy the Dead Sea was only sick.

George Burns

LIVE
LOVE
AND
LAST

People are always asking about the good old days. I say, why don't you say the good now days?

Robert M. Young

Seize the moment.
Remember all those
women on the *Titanic*
who waved off the
dessert cart.

Erma Bombeck

I know one should never say never, but I hope I'll get off the beach before the tide goes out.

Sir Terry Wogan on retirement

Life can only
be understood
backwards; but it must
be lived forwards.

Søren Kierkegaard

You only live once, but if you do it right, once is enough.

Mae West

And in the end it's not the
years in your life that count.
It's the life in your years.

Abraham Lincoln

There was no respect for youth when I was young, and now that I am old, there is no respect for age – I missed it coming and going.

J. B. Priestly

May you live all the
days of your life.

Jonathan Swift

Time doth flit; oh shit!

Dorothy Parker

You know you're getting old
when everything hurts. And
what doesn't hurt
doesn't work.

Hy Gardner

The key to successful ageing is to pay as little attention to it as possible.

Judith Regan

The problem with getting older is you still remember how things used to be.

Paul Newman

The old begin to complain
of the conduct of the young
when they themselves are
no longer able to set a
bad example.

François de La Rochefoucauld

Give me chastity and
continence, but
not yet.

Saint Aurelius Augustine

When you are dissatisfied
and would like to go back to
your youth, think of algebra.

Will Rogers

ILLS
PILLS
AND
TWINGES

As you get older three things happen. The first is your memory goes, and I can't remember the other two...

Norman Wisdom

I don't feel old. I don't
feel anything till noon.
That's when it's time
for my nap.

Bob Hope

My doctor told me to do something that puts me out of breath, so I've taken up smoking again.

Jo Brand

After you're older, two
things are possibly
more important than
any others: health
and money.

Helen Gurley Brown

Advanced old age is when
you sit in a rocking chair
and can't get it going.

Eliakim Katz

I don't do alcohol any more – I get the same effect just standing up fast.

Anonymous

I'm at an age when my back
goes out more than I do.

Phyllis Diller

I'm pushing 60. That's enough exercise
for me.

Mark Twain

Passing the vodka bottle and playing the guitar.

Keith Richards on how he keeps fit

Don't let ageing get you down. It's too hard to get back up.

John Wagner

When you become
senile, you won't
know it.

Bill Cosby

Never worry about your
heart till it stops beating.

E. B. White

Everything slows
down with age, except
the time it takes cake
and ice cream to
reach your hips.

John Wagner

They say that age is all
in your mind. The trick is
keeping it from creeping
down into your body.

Anonymous

If you rest, you rust.

Helen Hayes

A healthy old fellow, who is not a fool, is the happiest creature living.

Richard Steele

The years between 50 and 70 are the hardest. You are always being asked to do more, and you are not yet decrepit enough to turn them down.

T. S. Eliot

CHIN
UP
CHEST
OUT

I'm not sixty,
I'm 'sexty'!

Dolly Parton

I don't plan to grow old
gracefully; I plan to have
facelifts until my ears meet.

Rita Rudner

Middle age is when a narrow
waist and a broad mind
begin to change places.

Anonymous

I have a furniture problem. My chest has fallen into my drawers.

Billy Casper

I've only got one wrinkle and I'm sitting on it.

Jeanne Calment

Let us respect grey hairs,
especially our own.

J. P. Sears

Looking 50 is great –
if you're 60.

Joan Rivers

Some people, no matter how old they get, never lose their beauty – they merely move it from their faces into their hearts.

Martin Buxbaum

You can only perceive
real beauty in a
person as they
get older.

Anouk Aimée

There is more felicity on the far side of baldness than young men can possibly imagine.

Logan Pearsall Smith

Experience is a comb
that life gives you after
you lose your hair.

Judith Stern

Inflation is when you pay
15 dollars for the 10-dollar
haircut you used to get for
five dollars when you
had hair.

Sam Ewing

To win back my youth…
there is nothing I wouldn't
do – except take exercise,
get up early, or be a useful
member of the community.

Oscar Wilde

Years may wrinkle the skin, but to give up enthusiasm wrinkles the soul.

Samuel Ullman

An archaeologist is the best
husband any woman can
have: the older she gets, the
more interested he is in her.

Agatha Christie

Time may be a great
healer, but it's a
lousy beautician.

Anonymous

Don't retouch my wrinkles in the photograph. I would not want it to be thought that I had lived for all these years without something to show for it.

The Queen Mother

How foolish to think
that one can ever
slam the door in the
face of age. Much
wiser to be polite and
gracious and ask him
to lunch in advance.

Noël Coward

KEEP
CALM
AND
DRINK
UP

KEEP CALM AND DRINK UP

£4.99

ISBN: 978 1 84953 102 3

'*In victory, you deserve champagne; in defeat, you need it.*'

Napoleon Bonaparte

BAD ADVICE FOR GOOD PEOPLE.

Keep Calm and Carry On, a World War Two government poster, struck a chord in recent difficult times when a stiff upper lip and optimistic energy were needed again. But in the long run it's a stiff drink and flowing spirits that keep us all going.

Here's a book packed with proverbs and quotations showing the wisdom to be found at the bottom of the glass.

www.summersdale.com

KEEP CALM YOU'RE ONLY 60

KEEP CALM YOU'RE ONLY 60

KEEP CALM YOU'RE ONLY 60

KEEP CALM YOU'RE ONLY 60

KEEP CALM YOU'RE ONLY 60

KEEP CALM YOU'RE ONLY 60

KEEP CALM YOU'RE ONLY 60

KEEP CALM YOU'RE ONLY 60

KEEP CALM YOU'RE ONLY 60

KEEP CALM YOU'RE ONLY 60

KEEP CALM YOU'RE ONLY 60

KEEP CALM YOU'RE ONLY 60

KEEP CALM YOU'RE ONLY 60

KEEP CALM YOU'RE ONLY 60

KEEP CALM YOU'RE ONLY 60